A Networked Research Approach

A guide to conducting research in a network setting

ACKNOWLEDGMENTS

We would firstly like to acknowledge and thank Priyanthi Fernando, former Executive Secretary of the IFRTD Secretariat, who pioneered the Networked Research Approach. We also gratefully acknowledge the many participants in our networked research programmes past and future, and our donors; the Swiss Agency for Development and Cooperation (SDC), the Swedish International Development Cooperation Agency (Sida), the UK Department for International Development (DFID) and also the World Bank, who have promoted networked research not only through the provision of funding but through their support and participation.

A special thank you goes to Thomas Zeller (Deputy Director a.i. Thematic and Technical Resources Department at SDC) who has helped us to 'spread the word' about networked research and to Manuel Flury (Head of Thematic Service Knowledge and Research at SDC) for his feedback on the approach.

We are grateful to SDC for providing the financial support that has enabled us to develop this Manual in a participatory and networked manner. We could not have done this without the assistance, inputs and commitment of Skat (especially Urs Egger), Bellanet, the participants of the Mobility and Health Networked Research Programme, and the members and friends of IFRTD who attended a peer-assist workshop in Tanzania. Thank you and we hope we have been able to reflect your opinions and enthusiasm accurately.

The IFRTD Secretariat

A Networked Research Approach

A guide to conducting research in a network setting

Kate Czuczman

Practical
ACTION
PUBLISHING

Practical Action Publishing Ltd
25 Albert Street, Rugby, CV21 2SD, Warwickshire, UK
www.practicalactionpublishing.com

© Intermediate Technology Publications 2006

First published 2006\Digitised 2013

ISBN 13 Paperback: 9781853396618
ISBN Library Ebook: 9781780441511
Book DOI: http://dx.doi.org/10.3362/9781780441511

A catalogue record for this book is available from the British Library.

The authors, contributors and/or editors have asserted their rights under
the Copyright Designs and Patents Act 1988 to be identified as authors of
their respective contributions.

Since 1974, Practical Action Publishing has published and disseminated
books and information in support of international development work
throughout the world. Practical Action Publishing is a trading name
of Practical Action Publishing Ltd (Company Reg. No. 1159018), the
wholly owned publishing company of Practical Action. Practical Action
Publishing trades only in support of its parent charity objectives and any
profits are covenanted back to Practical Action (Charity Reg. No. 247257,
Group VAT Registration No. 880 9924 76).

CONTENTS

The inspiration for this approach

came from a philosophy of knowledge that is inclusive and democratic, and which challenges accepted hierarchies of knowledge production. Networked Research recognises the value of knowledge residing in the work experience of people dealing with complex development issues on a day to day basis, and aims to combine this knowledge with the rigour of research practice.

By bringing practitioners from different contexts and researchers together in a single project, the approach has allowed for fresh perspectives and locally relevant knowledge to emerge, has strengthened South-South and South-North partnerships, and has influenced the direction of change.

Priyanthi Fernando
Executive Director, Centre for
Poverty Analysis, Sri Lanka. 2006

A.0
INTRODUCTION

Welcome to the **Networked Research Approach**, a hands-on guide to conducting research in a network setting, developed by the International Forum for Rural Transport and Development (IFRTD). We have been using this approach for over eight years, in which time it has enabled us to bridge the divides between research, the communication of research findings and the realisation of change in development policy and practice. It has also helped us to establish mechanisms to sustain our research messages beyond the finite cycles of project funding, and to challenge the Northern bias of the international development research agenda.

Through this guide we will share with you our experiences applying the **Networked Research Approach** - the successes, the challenges, and the lessons that we have learnt. We hope that you will find our journey interesting and will be able to integrate some of this approach into your own work.

> While there has been extensive research in a variety of development sectors from natural resources to governance many in the development community, including practitioners and policymakers, feel removed from this research work, feeling that it has little impact on the reality of poverty"
>
> N Perkins et al,
> Healthlink, 2006

CORE VALUES OF NETWORKED RESEARCH
- South to South exchange.
- Research to leverage change.
- Continual learning.
- Peer support.
- Access to knowledge for all.
- Diversity enriches research.
- The research *process* is as critical as its outputs.
- Researchers are self-reflective.
- Research data is fed back to the field.
- Dissemination is targeted and interactive.

NETWORKED RESEARCH IS NOT...
- A methodology for research.
- A cost-effective mechanism to gather field data for analysis by Northern research institutions.
- An hierarchical top down approach.
- Prescriptive.

Networked Research is a *framework for conducting development research* that builds ownership, communication, and advocacy into the overall design of the research programme. Through this process-oriented approach international researchers are given the opportunity to work together to a common analytical framework, to cross-pollinate one another's work, to complement each other's research capacities and to participate in the synthesis and bringing together of the key issues.

Networked Research has demonstrated several significant impacts:

- It encourages ownership of research and findings at local, national and international level.

- It enables Southern stakeholders to contribute to and engage with the *international* development agenda.

- It creates sustainable multi-disciplinary Communities of Practice around research issues.

- It builds research capacity and challenges traditional perceptions of who is capable of carrying out research.

- It harnesses local knowledge and experience.

- It stimulates debate and raises awareness of research issues at local, national and international level.

- It commits a wide range of stakeholders to the resolution of specific research issues.

Despite the rhetoric of bottom-up development, the international development agenda remains dominated by the economic interests and institutional priorities of the North and supported by knowledge generated through Northern universities, resource centres and think tanks. One means of addressing this imbalance is to ensure that the research used to determine and justify development priorities is both Southern-driven and accessible to Southern-based policymakers and development practitioners. It is now recognised that it is no longer justifiable for development research to *primarily* be carried out by highly paid Northern researchers, and/or to sit on shelves gathering dust in academic or donor offices.

The **Networked Research Approach** was pioneered by the IFRTD, a Southern-driven global network of individuals and organisations with a rural access and mobility focus. As a network IFRTD is mandated to carry out research when members have identified significant gaps in knowledge that restrict their ability to advocate or implement change. The **Networked Research Approach** evolved from IFRTD's need to conduct this research in a way that fully reflects its Southern-driven networking principles.

LEVERAGING CHANGE

Networked Research can create a powerful groundswell for change. It generates a variety of new and related initiatives, builds capacity, and establishes new Communities of Practice capable of forming common advocacy strategies. Since initiating our first Networked Research programme in 1998 *(see Annex I)* IFRTD has witnessed the impact of this approach from the grassroots through to the international arena.

1. **Local:** The *Balancing the Load programme* on gender and transport included a case study on the Nkone river bridge in Meru district, Kenya, and its impact on travel and marketing activities for the local community. During his research the case study researcher was able to publicise the transport challenges faced by this isolated community and mobilise them to affect change. Today, as a result of this action research the Nkone bridge has been built, facilitating access to market centres, hospitals, churches and schools throughout the year.

2. **International:** The *GATNET Gender and Transport Community of Practice* began as an email network for researchers participating in the *Integrating Gender into World Bank Financed Transport Programmes* project. When the project finished in 2003 the 10 researchers decided to open their network to the public and today this email discussion list is a lively forum for debate and information sharing with over 100 members. The founding members still play a vital role, motivating discussions, and moderating virtual forums. GATNET has also become a recognised source of gender and transport expertise. In 2006 the World Bank solicited a consultation with the GATNET community to source inputs to their transport sector strategy (2007-2015) and the community has successfully lobbied for three special editions on gender in a leading transport journal.

Networked Research Programmes channel more research funding to developing countries and provide interesting projects that are meaningful in the local context.

The Networked Research Approach has been successfully pioneered and tested by IFRTD and ensures that research is relevant to and used by poor people and the organisations that work with and for them."

Thomas Zeller, Deputy Director a.i. Thematic and Technical Resource Department, SDC

> "The technique comes neither from rocket science nor some pious evangelical belief, but from some quite determined application of basic guiding principles that are the cornerstone of participative development"
>
> Megan Lloyd Laney, Communications Consultant and facilitator for the Waterways and Livelihoods Networked Research programme (see Annex I)

Utilising an existing network with established processes for identifying a Southern agenda **helps to ensure that the research is genuinely Southern-driven.**

The breadth of stakeholders that a network is able to bring into the research team **enriches the findings through the cross pollination of perspectives, experiences and skills** across geographical, language and institutional barriers.

The network environment **encourages accountability and transparency** among and between peer researchers and the core team.

The global nature of the programme **validates the activities of individual researchers,** facilitating promotional activities and opening doors to dialogue with change makers.

Continuous, interactive information sharing and advocacy **provides a guarantee that research will be used** and won't gather dust on shelves.

examples and **useful hints**

A.3 WHO IS THIS MANUAL FOR?

This manual is for individuals or organisations looking to maximise the impact of their research in a development context. It introduces the **Networked Research Approach** and through a series of steps, examples and useful hints (❶), guides you in the implementation of your own **Networked Research** Programme.

It will provide valuable inputs to:

- Networks and Non Governmental Organisations (NGOs) mandated to carry out action or participative research to support an evidence base for advocacy activities.
- Researchers and research institutions that wish to broaden stakeholder participation and optimise the impact of their research programmes.
- Potential funders of **Networked Research** programmes who wish to gain a greater understanding of the approach.
- Individuals and organisations with an interest in participative methodologies and research for development.
- Members of the IFRTD network and Secretariat who will participate in future **Networked Research** programmes.

Examples in this manual are drawn from IFRTD's experience applying the **Networked Research Approach** in an international context within the transport and development sector. It can however also be translated for use with other sectors and issues, and applied to smaller regional or national programmes *(see the boxed example below)*.

It (Networked Research) broadens the scope and provides comparative data sets in regional and global scales within a common timeframe, this is unique."

Kate Molesworth, Reproductive Health and Social Development Advisor, Swiss Tropical Institute, also core team member, Mobility and Health Programme, 2006.

BALANCING THE LOAD

"What I really liked about it [Networked Research in the *Balancing the Load programme*] was that it brought in and supported new people with strong field experience, who didn't necessarily have a conventional academic research training or regular access to recent research findings. I thought *Balancing the Load* was brilliant from that perspective. It made me think about the research potential of a wider policy and practitioner community.

Dr Gina Porter, Senior Research Fellow in the Department of Anthropology, Durham University and research participant in Balancing the Load *(see Annex I)*

Since participating in *Balancing the Load* Gina has incorporated the principles of Networked Research into a number of research projects. For example it was used in a UK Department for International Development (DFID) funded project to widen the food marketing policy evidence base in Nigeria. 15 researchers across Nigeria's major regions participated, incorporating syntheses of previous studies with new field research and ultimately collaborating to develop a comprehensive set of policy recommendations.

Photo courtesy of Paul Starkey

THE NETWORKED RESEARCH FRAMEWORK

This guide is organised into four simple steps, walking you through an example **Networked Research** programme from the identification of your research issue(s) to leaving behind a dynamic Community of Practice when the research funding ends. An overview of this framework is given below and in figure A.4.

STEP 1

Getting Started

Laying the foundation for a good **Networked Research** programme; identifying your research issue(s) and objective(s), establishing your team and putting effective networking processes in place.

STEP 2

Developing your Research Framework

Bringing together the entire research team to define your analytical research framework, terms of reference and local and international dissemination and advocacy strategies.

STEP 3

Research Phase

Concentrating on strengthening networking processes to build research capacity and ultimately deliver high quality research outputs. There is a continued focus on ongoing advocacy activities.

STEP 4

Impact and Sustainability

Synthesising and communicating your research findings to maximum effect. Delivering the right message to the right audience(s) at the right time and establishing a sustainable Community of Practice to take the issues forward.

A.4 A SUGGESTED FRAMEWORK FOR NETWORKED RESEARCH

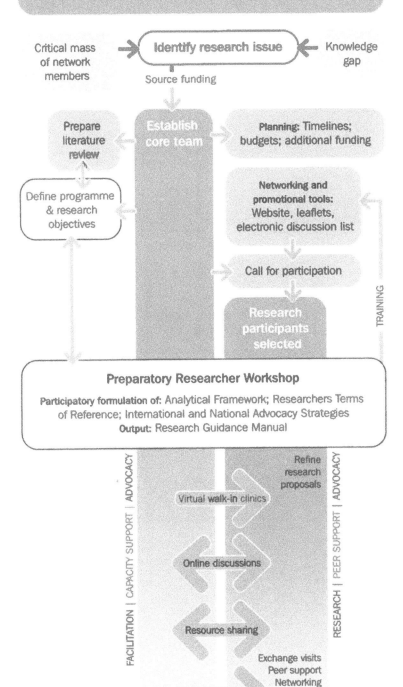

Promote the research internationally

Develop literature review

Promote the research locally, nationally and internationally

Engage new stakeholders at local and national level

Further develop literature review

Report writing
Peer review; translation; dissemination

Researcher Synthesis Workshop

Sharing; learning; synthesis; analysis
Outputs: Case studies; key recommendations; common platform

Wider audience

Final (International) Symposium

Informed Policymakers and Practioners

Sustainable Community of Practice

Targeted Information Products

New Recommendations for Policy and Practice

New Recommendations for Follow-up Research

New Relationships Established Between Researchers and Decision makers

1.0
STEP 1 | GETTING STARTED

In this step you will lay the foundation for a good **Networked Research** programme, identifying your issue(s) and objective(s), forming your team, planning and budgeting the activities, and establishing the tools that you will use to communicate both internally and with the wider development community.

IDENTIFYING YOUR RESEARCH ISSUE

Southern based networks are ideally positioned to identify research priorities because they are close to the real issues on the ground and provide a mechanism for gathering a critical mass of interested stakeholders.

Sourcing funding for a research programme that is not donor or research council led but truly responsive to a Southern agenda can require sustained lobbying over a number of years. For an example see the box on page 10. Get started by using the tools already available within your network to raise awareness of your research issue. Ideas could include:

- Initiating virtual discussions on electronic discussion lists, blogs and websites.
- Initiating face-to-face discussions at meetings, workshops and conferences.
- Commissioning and disseminating opinion pieces or position papers.
- Utilising the local media (radio, print publications, television).
- Consolidating existing information to identify issues and reveal knowledge gaps.
- Recognising and supporting 'champions' who are active on the issue(s) within your network.

- ISSUES
- OBJECTIVES
- ROLES
- RESPONSIBILITIES
- BUDGETS
- TIMELINES
- PARTICIPANT SELECTION
- ORGANISATION
- NETWORKING

What is a blog?

A blog is a website where entries are made in journal style. They often provide commentary or news on a specific subject. A typical blog combines text, images, and links to other blogs, web pages, and related media. The ability for readers to leave comments in an interactive format is an important feature of most blogs.
www.en.wikipedia.org /wiki/Blog

FOR EXAMPLE... FROM NETWORK PRIORITY TO RESEARCH PRIORITY (1996-2002)

1996: The importance of rural waterways as a means of accessing basic services for many of the world's poorest and most isolated communities was first raised within the IFRTD network via its newsletter.

1997: The issue was then addressed at a workshop hosted by an IFRTD affiliated network in Bangladesh.

1998: The IFRTD together with the Rural Travel and Transport Program for Sub-Saharan Africa (RTTP) commissioned a small scoping study that produced a position paper 'Inland Waterways and Rural Transport'. Following the publication of this paper the IFRTD lobbied international donors for funding to initiate new research and raise visibility of the issue.

2002: This proposal was picked up by DFID's Engineering Knowledge and Research (KaR) programme. *Waterways and Livelihoods* became IFRTD's second international **Networked Research** programme *(see Annex 1).*

SOUTHERN-LED?

Ironically, although research is a means of pushing the boundaries of our knowledge, finding funding to research issues outside of the mainstream discourse is difficult. For example in the transport sector, gaining acceptance (and funds) for gender and transport research, or research on rural waterways, required a mixture of luck and persistence!

Most often, funding for research is generated in Northern countries, and even where efforts are made to develop research capacity in the 'South', the topics prioritised are those that are of interest to the funders. Southern research organisations, strapped as they often are for cash, can sometimes collude in perpetuating this unequal partnership.

The primary objective of any **Networked Research** programme is to induce change that will lead to sustainable poverty reduction. To define your overall programme objective(s) you will therefore need to work with network members to identify:

What change(s) you wish to see?

What evidence/data you need to support the network to advocate for that change?

Research can be carried out in many ways but **Networked Research** is most suited to a social science approach that embraces a variety of perspectives. We recommend that you develop broad based research objectives that will give your researchers the flexibility to adapt their research. This will enable them to develop meaningful outputs for their local context while still providing the comparative evidence base required to advance international debate.

In the example below we demonstrate how the objectives defined for the recent *Mobility and Health Networked Research programme* bring together both the changes sought and the evidence base that will be established.

MOBILITY AND HEALTH

In 2004, in response to the practical activities of network members, the IFRTD mandated its Secretariat to explore the relationship between mobility and health in developing countries. The aim was to provide an overview of the situation in many different contexts, to highlight good practice and above all to enable both transport and health professionals to make informed choices with respect to improving access to health care in developing countries.

The broad based objectives developed for the programme are:

1. Increase the knowledge base on the relationship between mobility and the achievement of the health Millennium Development Goals.

2. Enable transport professionals to take an holistic, health-sensitive approach to the planning and implementation of transport interventions.

3. Sensitise the health sector to mobility and health issues.

Networks are powerful mechanisms for sharing inform-ation and knowledge. They also promote communication and coordination to achieve sustainable development. Networks act as effective catalysts for building up relation-ships and commitment among public and private stakeholders at local, national and international levels. They help build trustful relationships as a basis for sharing information and knowledge, and serve as mutual learning and capacity building mechanisms."

Work the Net,
A Management Guide
for Formal Networks,
GTZ, 2006

The role of the core team is to facilitate the overall programme, to provide multi-disciplinary technical inputs and to support the researchers with online, telephone or face-to-face guidance.

You should aim to form a multi-disciplinary, gender balanced core team that reflects the geography, and language demands of the overall programme. Ideally the initiating network should take on the coord-inating functions of the core team.

Good technical expertise is an important contribution of the core team to the **Networked Research** process. However this does not mean that all of the core team should be drawn from Northern institutions and effort should be made to identify and co-opt Southern technical experts. The core team should also include a member or members with strong communication skills to enable the programme to achieve its communication and advocacy objectives.

Team domination

Beware that the coordinating member of the core team does not dominate the group, particu-larly towards the end of the programme when the pressure to complete is high and the temptation is to become less participative.

CORE TEAM TASK CHECKLIST

This check-list is not exhaustive and should be carefully cross-referenced against the objectives of your own programme.

Programme Development

☐ Complete a literature review.

☐ Structure the programme networking tools (e.g interactive website, electronic discussion list).

☐ Structure the *Preparatory Researcher Workshop(s)*.

☐ Bring together and disseminate the analytical framework.

☐ Structure the *Researcher Synthesis Workshop* and *International Symposium*.

☐ Work on the synthesis and comparative analysis.

☐ Facilitate an international advocacy strategy.

☐ Align the programme to international development aims such as the Millennium Development Goals and national level poverty reduction strategies.

☐ Oversight and synthesis of monitoring and evaluation activities.

☐ Oversight of output quality.

Facilitation, Logistics and Promotion

☐ Set overall timetable and milestones and ensure deadlines are met.

☐ Report to donors in accordance with financing agreements.

☐ Provide clear definition of participant roles and responsibilities.

☐ Ensure that all expenses are covered by the budget and review cash-flow and expenditure.

☐ Publicise call for participation (where appropriate).

☐ Select, contract and manage the research team.

☐ Organise logistics for *Researcher Workshops (Preparatory and Synthesis)* and the *Final Symposium*.

☐ Compile *Research Guidance Manual* (Terms of Reference).

☐ Maintain the website/online team-space.

☐ Administration of the electronic discussion list.

☐ Oversee the production and dissemination of programme information outputs.

☐ Oversee translation of:

    (i) literature review

    (ii) Research Guidance Manual

    (iii) electronic discussion list contributions

    (iv) website

    (v) other information outputs

☐ Identify and pursue opportunities to promote the programme and findings.

☐ Promote the *Final Symposium*.

Capacity Building:

☐ Invest time in team building.

☐ Coordinate communication within the network.

☐ Provide the researchers with technical and logistical support.

☐ Facilitate peer review of case studies.

☐ Where necessary train the researchers in the use of communication tools e.g. phone calls over the Internet, electronic discussion lists, and online team-space/website.

A BALANCED TEAM

The core team for IFRTD's *Waterways and Livelihoods Networked Research programme* included:

- Regional staff members of the IFRTD network.
- A water transport specialist.
- An economist.
- A gender specialist.
- A communications specialist.

TEAM COMMUNICATION

It is important that all core team members are able to participate in the core team meetings to ensure equal ownership of the programme. Regular face-to-face meetings can be expensive, particularly if you ha achieved a good geographical balance in your core team. Allow additional budget for these meetings and innovate with communications tools such as:

- Video conferencing.
- Skype conferencing (telephone or instant messaging).
- Telephone conferencing.

CHALLENGES

Beware of the core team dominating the research programme. The cor team should delegate responsibilities and encourage researchers to tak leadership roles. For example:

- Researchers with good Internet access and aptitude could take on t responsibility for the facilitation of the electronic discussion list or the administration of the website.
- A researcher with a gender analysis specialism could watchdog the gender focus of the overall programme.

Introducing Skype

Skype is a Voice over Internet Protocol (VoIP) technology enabling low cost or free telephone connections over the Internet plus instant messaging.
www.skype.com

There is a symbiotic relationship between the definition of your research objectives and the findings from your literature review. Your objectives will guide your literature review, while the findings of your review will also help to refine and consolidate your objectives. This is illustrated in our visual representation of the **Networked Research** process on page 7.

A good literature review will:

- Signpost existing knowledge and experience.

- Identify what is known.

- Identify what is not known.

- Highlight controversial issues.

- Prompt new research questions.

One of the first tasks of your core team should be to complete and share the literature review.

Don't limit your literature review to an international web search. Remember that interesting literature may be available in a local context.

Your literature review is a work in progress. Encourage the researchers to complete supplementary reviews as the programme progresses, contributing to a comprehensive bibliography at the completion of the programme.

In the case of the *Mobility and Health* programme the bibliography is on the website and can be edited and added to by the researchers and core team at any time.
See *www.mobilityandhealth.org*

Gantt charts are
a useful tool for
timeline planning
www.ganttchart.com

1.5 TIMELINE

Often timelines are prepared by starting from a perceived deadline then working backwards and distributing milestones over time. A more realistic method is to:

1. Write down the tasks that have to be carried out until the project is completed.
2. Write down an estimation of the necessary time for each task.
3. Add to every task at least 30% of the time that you have estimated.
4. Analyse which tasks depend upon one another.
5. Use all of this information to develop your timeline.

The timeline example given below is based upon an international **Networked Research** programme involving 24 case study researchers. Please note that this is not a reflection of *actual time* taken to complete tasks but of the *windows of time* that could be assigned to each activity.

EXAMPLE TIMELINE

Establishing the core team, including the definition
of roles and responsibilities ....**4 weeks**

Develop, write and edit literature review ....**4 weeks**

Participant selection ....**8-16 weeks**

Development of website and electronic discussion list ....**4 weeks**

Preparation and organisation of
Preparatory Researcher Workshop(s) ....**4 weeks**

Editing, translation and dissemination
of **Research Guidance Manual** ....**2 weeks**

Develop contracts for researchers ....**1 week**

Execution of research case studies
plus technical support from core team ....**6-8 months**

Advocacy programme (including communications tools
– website, promotion etc) ....**continuous**

Preparation and organisation of
Researcher Synthesis Workshop ....**4 weeks**

Preparation of *International Symposium* ....**4-8 weeks**

Review of first draft of case studies ....**12 weeks**

Review of second draft of case studies......................**12 weeks**

Edit case studies for book, website, CD-Rom ....**20 weeks**

TOTAL: ....**107 weeks (2 years)**

king your research objectives as your starting point you will need
decide upon the optimum size for your **Networked Research**
ogramme. Consider:

The breadth of case studies needed to address your objectives.

The funds (potentially) available.

The capacity within the network to manage a **Networked Research**
programme.

There is no prescribed formula for budgeting a **Networked Research**
rogramme but we have compiled a basic checklist below that can be
dapted to suit your programme. Below this is a useful guideline to the
roportional division of a typical **Networked Research** budget.

Core Team Activities

☐ Time to coordinate core team and programme.

☐ Time to complete literature review.

☐ Time/expenses participating in core team meetings (4 per year).

☐ Time/expenses participating in *Preparatory Researcher
Workshop(s)*.

☐ Time/expenses participating in *Researcher Synthesis
Workshop* and *Final Symposium*.

☐ Time/expenses supporting researchers.

☐ Time on inputs to publications.

Researchers

☐ Research fee.

☐ Field expenses.

☐ Exchange visits.

☐ Advocacy activities e.g. stakeholder workshop(s).

☐ Cost of Internet access.

☐ Cost of report production and translation where necessary.

Developing and Maintaining Network Portal

☐ Website design.

☐ Website hosting.

☐ Website maintenance.

☐ Electronic discussion list charges (if applicable).

Researcher Workshops
(at least two – Preparatory and Synthesis)

- ☐ International and regional travel.
- ☐ Accommodation.
- ☐ Venue hire.
- ☐ Facilitator fee.
- ☐ Simultaneous translation (if required).
- ☐ Field visit logistics.
- ☐ Local organiser expenses.
- ☐ Materials.
- ☐ Local transport.
- ☐ Social event.

Programme wide Advocacy Activities

- ☐ Seed fund for small local level activities and conference participation.

Communications

- ☐ Brochures.
- ☐ Learning notes.
- ☐ Technical guides.
- ☐ CD-Rom.
- ☐ Book.
- ☐ Dissemination costs for brochures, CD Roms, books etc.
- ☐ Translation.

International Symposium

- ☐ International and regional travel.
- ☐ Accommodation.
- ☐ Venue hire.
- ☐ Facilitator.
- ☐ Simultaneous translation.
- ☐ Field visit costs.
- ☐ Local transport.
- ☐ Materials.
- ☐ Social event.

- ☐ **Monitoring and Evaluation**

- ☐ **Miscellaneous**

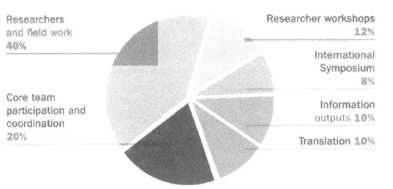

Researchers and field work 40%

Researcher workshops 12%

International Symposium 8%

Core team participation and coordination 20%

Information outputs 10%

Translation 10%

Carefully align your budget with your timeline. The **Networked Research** programme has proved to be 'front-loaded'. By which we mean there are many outgoings in the early stages, for example; website set-up, researcher fees, core team meetings, *Preparatory Researcher Workshop(s)*.

LESSONS LEARNED

1. Be clear and fair about the rate of disbursement for researcher fees and expenses. Researchers who are not based in institutions may not be able to carry the costs of field research against their first fee instalment if it is too low.

2. Include sufficient resources to coordinate the core team.

3. Ensure that there is a balance between resources available to the core team and the researchers.

4. Remember to allow for fluctuations in exchange rates.

LOST IN TRANSLATION

Translation is time consuming and costly but without it you will lose important South to South dialogue and the corresponding cross pollination of ideas and technologies from certain regions.

FOR EXAMPLE...

The *Waterways and Livelihoods research programme (see Annex I)* commissioned research in Latin America but due to donor funding restrictions the programme outputs could not be translated into Spanish. The researchers from Peru and Nicaragua alongside *Final Symposium* participants from Colombia were motivated by the new knowledge they had gained but were unable to motivate wider interest in their home countries due to a lack of Spanish language evidence and resources.

The methods we have used to select research participants have varied according to the objectives of the programmes. Where the aims have been to build a body of knowledge and raise awareness for a previously unexplored issue, for example *Balancing the Load* or *Mobility and Health*, then an open call for participation has been favoured. In the case of the *Waterways and Livelihoods* programme where specific comparative data was sought from particular locations, a more targeted selection process was adopted in which researchers were identified by the core team and invited to participate.

Other factors, such as the time and resources available, may affect your choice of selection method. An open call for participation and the associated proposal selection process is time consuming, but much more transparent.

CIRCULATING A CALL FOR PARTICIPATION

A call for participating researchers should be circulated as extensively as possible, utilising both print and electronic media – e.g. websites, electronic mailing lists, and print newsletters and bulletins. The emphasis should be on reaching as many Southern individuals and organisations as possible. Remember to use known contacts and 'word of mouth' or even 'word of email'.

Invite applicants to explain in their expression of interest how they will address the research issue within the context of their own work. This is important as it will indicate how the research findings will be used to leverage change. Extensive research experience should not be a prerequisite for applicants, however applicants must be able to commit their time and adhere to the core values of **Networked Research**.

Depending upon the time available and the expected response rate the participant selection process could be staggered to include up to four stages, for example:

- Submission of proposal abstracts.

- Short-listing by core team.

- Submission of full proposals by short-listed candidates.

- Selection by core team.

Give clear guidance regarding the required content of both abstracts and full proposals, this should be based upon your selection criteria *(see page 21)*.

Remuneration and disbursement schedules should be stated clearly from the beginning of the process, preferably in the call for participation, to avoid confusion further down the line.

CHALLENGES:

1. Northern research institutions can unconsciously become a bottleneck for the participation of Southern practitioners in development research. During the call for participation for the *Mobility and Health* Networked Research programme *(see Annex I)* the core team encountered a repeated reluctance to share the call with Southern partners for lack of confidence in their capacity to participate. **Check that Northern institutions are circulating the call with their Southern networks and partners.**

2. Non Governmental Organisations (NGOs), Community Based Organisations (CBOs) and networks, may lack confidence in their research capacity, particularly in the context of an international programme. **The call for participation should provide clear guidance on application eligibility, expectations of previous research experience, and the level of support available to participants within the programme.**

3. Grassroots NGOs, CBOs and networks may not be connected to the information networks that carry and circulate postings on research calls. **The core team should research potential participants and solicit applications directly where appropriate – be clear that this does not guarantee selection.**

Allow plenty of time for the call for participation to reach new audiences. Plan for bulletin and newsletter print-runs and allow time for dissemination and response.

Collaborative multi-disciplinary applications should be welcomed. Where interest is shown from Northern research institutions they should be encouraged to collaborate with Southern organisations or individuals. The roles and responsibilities will need to be clearly outlined and the bulk of the work and the responsibility should reside with the Southern partner.

PARTICIPANT SELECTION

The core team will select the research participants from the short-listed applications. You may already have some criteria set by your programme objectives or the requirements of your funders. For example, the number of researchers or the number of countries that should be included. Other important criteria to be considered in the selection process include:

☐ The research should not stand on its own and it should be shown how it will fit into a wider body of work or build upon existing research.

☐ Good diversity between the research proposals, providing the comparative data required by your programme e.g. geographical or thematic diversity.

Good ideas
Don't just look for good proposals. Look also for good ideas, particularly those coming from practitioners and the grassroots.

☐ Balance between academic and community based or practitioner researchers.

☐ Gender awareness (including gender disaggregated data).

☐ Awareness of other vulnerable groups e.g. people with disabilities, people living with HIV/AIDS, refugees, the elderly.

☐ Gender balance among researchers.

☐ A clear strategy for advocacy and dissemination, or demonstrable interest in this aspect of the programme.

☐ Interest in networking and information sharing.

☐ Demonstrable linkages to international development targets (e.g. Millennium Development Goals). This may not be appropriate where the **Networked Research** is highlighting an issue that challenges the international development agenda.

AVOID A CLASH OF IDEOLOGIES

While participant diversity is one of the strengths of **Networked Research**, widely differing ideologies can sometimes have negative consequences. For example in a **Networked Research** programme that included both academics and activists, the academic researchers were unable to adopt the full participatory research methodology developed by the activists due to programmatic, contextual and financial constraints. This led to considerable tension and resulted in the rejection of the final research outputs by the activists.

WORKING TOGETHER

At this stage the core team is in a position to identify synergies between applications and/or complementarities between researchers' capacity that suggest advantages in merging specific project proposals. In this situation, dialogue, transparency and sensitivity are required to ensure that both the core team and the researchers are happy with the decision. The core team must clearly convey:

• The comparative advantages of merging.

• The potential complementarities and reasons for integration.

• The need to work together to establish new roles, responsibilities and resource allocation.

MOBILITY AND HEALTH

The *Mobility and Health Networked Research programme* experienced both positive and negative outcomes from the merger of applicants' proposals.

In Latin America two applicants from the same country submitted similar proposals, one a consultant with considerable research experience and the other from a CBO with excellent relationships with local stakeholders. After careful discussions about roles and responsibilities a merged proposal was developed which will strengthen both the skills and expertise of the two researchers and deliver a dynamic case study for the programme.

In comparison in Africa a similar merger did not go so smoothly. Despite the synergies and complementarities of the two proposals, after some discussion the researchers declined to collaborate. This was in part due to a difficult working relationship between the researchers and in part due to a lack of clarity from the core team in explaining the rational for the merger and the new division of roles, responsibilities and resources that it would entail.

CAPACITY BUILDING

Capacity building is one of the core values of **Networked Research**. For this reason it is important to look for potential as well as previous experience in the applications. The overall programme will struggle however if many participants are weak in the same areas. So look to achieve a balance.

Once you have identified your selection criteria it is possible to develop an objective rating system that all members of the core team can use to impartially select the research participants. Be careful to incorporate an opportunity for qualitative feedback to capture the 'potential' in applications that may not score highly in aspects relating to research skills and experience.

WHO IS A RESEARCHER?

Networked Research challenges traditional perceptions of who is capable of carrying out research and how it should be done. Research is often seen as a professional research activity that should be carried out by those trained in particular disciplines. Quantitative analysis and 'objectivity' are valued over qualitative and intuitive knowledge.

IFRTD's **Networked Research** has demonstrated that with few external inputs people without the 'professional training' but with close links to the subjects of research are able to engage closely with the issues that affect them or the people they work with on a day to day basis.

The external inputs (core team support, peer assist) are valuable for enabling these people to locate their practical experiences within overarching analytical frameworks, to be able to take a fresh perspective on what they do, and to use this analysis to make changes in their own work or that of others.

Networked Research challenges professional researchers to collaborate with a new generation of researchers who add value through their local knowledge, existing relationships with change makers, and fresh perspectives grounded in practical reality.

Create an appealing public image for your research programme, for example a logo, strapline and a clear mission statement. This is the user-friendly face of your research and will help to engage new audiences. Remember that not everyone that you need on board to leverage change will be interested from the outset.

This does not need to be expensive – NGOs can often provide quality photographs to illustrate your issues, print and web design students (or even professionals) may do pro-bono work. (*See Annex II for examples of the public personas of previous IFRTD Networked Research programmes.*)

BRANDING YOUR RESEARCH

For the *Waterways and Livelihoods Networked Research programme* the official funding title of 'A Comparative Assessment of the Operational Characteristics of Rural Water Transport' became the brand featured to the left.

1.9 CREATING AN ONLINE NETWORKING HUB

With a geographically dispersed team the tools that you use for communication will need to be well planned, accessible to all, and should where possible, facilitate multi-person dialogue rather than one-to-one exchanges.

WEBSITE OR ONLINE TEAM SPACE

Develop a website that will serve as an information and networking hub for the researchers. The website will host:

- Details about the programme.
- The literature review.
- Additional information resources related to the research theme(s).
- Relevant web links.
- Relevant policy guidelines.
- The **Research Guidance Manual** (Terms of Reference).

The website will also become a promotional tool for the research programme and the issues concerned. It should be user friendly and accessible, with easily downloadable resources.

Free image resources:

Photoshare is a service of the INFO programme, helping international non-profits to communicate health and development issues through photography. Free images can be requested from an extensive photo database for non-profit educational use. *www.photoshare.org*

The Flickr Creative Commons A searchable public photo-sharing database. A proportion of images are available for free reproduction under 'creative commons' licenses. *www.flickr.com/creativecommons*

*Interactive Training,
Mobility and Health
Programme 2006*

ELECTRONIC DISCUSSION LIST

The core team will also establish an electronic discussion list as a means
of facilitating communication between the entire research team. It is
important to foster 'ownership' of this email list among the researchers
and to encourage a spirit of free and open discussion.

In a previous IFRTD **Networked Research** programme the participation of the programme donor in the electronic discussion list meant that
the researchers did not feel comfortable sharing their challenges and
questions and eventually information sharing stopped and discussions
became bilateral between the researchers and individual members of the
core team. The consequence was lost learning and less transparency.
The current *Mobility and Health* programme, which also includes
a donor as part of the core team, has attempted to overcome this
situation by ensuring that the donor participates fully in the researcher
workshops and becomes a known and valued member of the team.

Again there are free resources available – electronic discussion lists
and blogs are available online, and the website could be hosted within
the existing website of one of the core team members or developed
using a low cost hub site, for example 'Teamspace'.

USEFUL RESOURCES:

- **www.blogger.com** : Free online blog space.

- **www.Dgroups.org** : Online platform for international networking (includes electronic mailing list). The following organisations are entitled to use Dgroups: Partner organisations or members of Bellanet, CGIAR, CTA, DFID, Hivos, ICA, ICCO, IICD, KIT, OneWorld, UNAIDS, CIDA, Danida, FAO, IDRC, INASP, SNV, Sida, SDC, UNECA, and World Bank.

- **www.groups.yahoo.com / www.groups.google.com** : Free electronic mailing list services.

- **www.babelfish.altavista.com** : Free online translation tool useful for email correspondence.

- **www.teamspace.com** : Low cost and easy to use web portal.

- **www.skype.com** : Voice over Internet Protocol (VoIP) technology enabling low cost or free telephone connections over the Internet plus instant messaging.

THE DIGITAL DIVIDE

The **Networked Research Approach** has developed in an international context in which it has become reliant upon electronic means of communication. We recognise that extensive use of web portals, blogs and electronic mailing lists to facilitate networking may be exclusionary and contrary to the inclusive values of **Networked Research.**

The level of inclusiveness you must achieve depends on your objectives and who you wish to work with. The more you go beyond those with easy access to the Internet, to those who have easy access only to email, to those who have only difficult access to email, the more you will need to invest in other forms of networking - face-to-face meetings, support visits, telephone calls, resourcing access to email/Internet; and this must be reflected in your budget and the support you provide to researchers. The added value of such an investment however, may be considerable!

Web protocol
Where applicable it is important to establish a protocol for translation in relation to the web-portal and the list-serv:

- What will be translated?

- Who will carry out the translations?

- How quickly will translations be completed?

- How will translators be alerted?

27

2.0
STEP 2 | DEVELOPING THE RESEARCH FRAMEWORK

The participative formulation of the research framework is one of the pillars of the **Networked Research Approach**. It encourages ownership of research and findings and lays the foundation for a geographically dispersed team to work collaboratively from the outset.

2.1 PREPARATORY RESEARCHER WORKSHOP

- BUILDING BONDS
- ANALYTICAL FRAMEWORK
- TERMS OF REFERENCE
- REFINING PROPOSALS
- ADVOCACY STRATEGY

To initiate the programme the selected researchers are brought together in a **Preparatory Researcher Workshop**. Depending upon the size of the research programme this will either be one international workshop or a series of regional workshops. The objectives of the **Preparatory Researcher Workshop(s)** are to:

- Lay a foundation for good networking.
- Establish trust and an open attitude for learning from one another.
- Agree collective and individual research and advocacy objectives.
- Collaboratively define the analytical framework and agree on a common terminology.
- Collaboratively develop the Terms of Reference for the researchers.
- Identify strengths and gaps in the research and advocacy capacities of the researchers.
- Peer-review and refine final research proposals or develop research design (where proposals were not the basis for the selection of researchers).
- Develop a common understanding of the principles of **Networked Research**, including communication and advocacy.

The primary outputs from this workshop will be the analytical framework and Terms of Reference for the researchers. These will be collated in a **Research Guidance Manual** that will be shared with all researchers in conjunction with their contracts or letters of agreement.

When a series of **Preparatory Researcher Workshops** is necessary they should be held in progression to enable continuity of the human

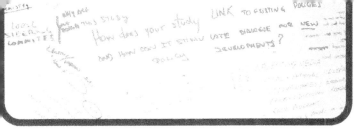

Thoughts shared at a World Café (see page 31)

resource inputs such as facilitation and technical expertise. This will also enable the progressive development of your research framework and the **Research Guidance Manual**.

WHO SHOULD PARTICIPATE?

The newly selected research team should attend the **Preparatory Researcher Workshop** alongside members of the core team who will provide organisational and technical inputs. In the case of a series of regional meetings at least one core team member should attend all workshops for the purpose of continuity. Where possible the technical resource persons should also attend all workshops, although there may be language constraints to this.

WORKSHOP LOCATION

Ideally the workshop will be hosted in one of the focal research locations by a member of the new research team. This has the advantage of creating an atmosphere at the workshop that is closer to the atmosphere in which the research will be conducted. It also provides opportunities, if necessary, to brainstorm research questions with key stakeholders (e.g. government officials or key persons from the community) or to pilot test research tools (e.g. a focus group check list or a household questionnaire).

To facilitate this you can request that the researchers bid for the opportunity to host the **Preparatory Researcher Workshop**. Factors to consider when choosing the location will include:

- What are the comparative travel and accommodation costs?

- Does the local researcher/research team have institutional and organisational support?

- What is the potential for organising an interesting field visit?

- How does the researcher plan to maximise this opportunity to promote their planned research at local (maybe national) level?

- Does the available venue present a good working space that will motivate team spirit?

- If possible an Internet connection should be available to enable training on the use of the team website and online research.

LOCAL ORGANISING TEAM

The local organising team should be well briefed by the core team and the facilitator well in advance of the workshop. The local organising team will be responsible for:

- Organising participant travel, accommodation and visas.
- Organising the workshop venue.
- Remuneration of participant expenses.
- Organising the field visit logistics.
- Identifying special guests and organising their attendance.
- Organising a social event in the evening!

WORKSHOP FACILITATION

Recruitment of a good facilitator is vital to the success of your **Preparatory Researcher Workshop**. Their use of innovative techniques will maximise this opportunity to establish good networking bonds amongst the researchers. The facilitator should have a good grasp of the issues and be able to make sure that the knowledge arising from the different perspectives represented is brought out (including the knowledge of the core team). The facilitator will work with the core team and the local organising team to plan and facilitate the workshop and should have the language capacity to facilitate a multi-lingual international workshop or, for continuity, a series of regional workshops.
See Annex III for a facilitator's check list.

WORKSHOP GROUNDRULES

Workshop groundrules should be defined by the participants at the beginning of the workshop and displayed prominently throughout, increasing ownership and consciousness. Good workshop groundrules might include:

- Constructive criticism.
- Self reflection.
- Informal atmosphere.
- Open attitudes.
- Listening.

POTENTIAL WORKSHOP SESSIONS

There are many innovative techniques that can be used to stimulate networking between participants and at the same time achieve the specific objectives and desired outputs of your workshop. We have listed here some suggestions of sessions that we have used and found to be successful.

The participating researcher should not be a member of the local organising team as this will impede her/his full participation in the workshop.

The use of a core team member as the workshop facilitator should be avoided as this can lead to domination by the core team.

This is a session characterised by a series of simultaneous conversations answering pre-determined questions. The participants change tables during the process and focus on identifying shared points of view in response to each question. One person remains at the table as the 'host' to maintain the thread of the discussion. Advantages of including a World Café session include:

- Fostering open and meaningful discussion on a topic and highlighting shared perspectives.

- Involving people, particularly those meeting for the first time, in meaningful conversation.

World Café sessions were used at the *Mobility and Health Preparatory Researcher Workshops* to help to develop the data collection tools and questionnaires for the analytical framework. The researchers rotated from table to table brainstorming a diverse range of concepts and indicators which were then brought together in a plenary session.

Useful weblink
www.worldcafe.com

Presentation at the Case Study Gallery

POTENTIAL WORKSHOP SESSIONS > Case Study Gallery

This is a recommended method that enables researchers to share their project proposals with their peers in an informal setting, avoiding a series of lengthy presentations.

Researchers display a poster identifying the core components of their research and if possible additional photographs and other visual aids. These posters should be displayed in an informal setting with plenty of space. It is a good idea to organise this session immediately after a coffee break and serve refreshments in the same area to give the participants plenty of time to move around reading and absorbing the posters.

Each researcher then makes a brief five minute presentation of their research proposal to their fellow participants, highlighting their 'wants', 'needs' and 'strengths'. For the researchers this session will help to underscore where and how they can assist one another and for the core team it is an opportunity to identify where capacity gaps might be.

The core team should also make a presentation on their contributions to the overall programme, highlighting their 'wants' and 'needs' and the motivation for their participation. This will help the researchers to understand the role of the core team and the support that they can pro-vide. It will also demonstrate how the core team will be able to add value to their own work through their participation in the programme.

POTENTIAL WORKSHOP SESSIONS > **Rotating Peer-Assist**

This is a session in which the researchers will work with one another on a one-to-one basis to gain new knowledge and insights on their proposal. The benefits of a peer-assist session are that it:

- Builds trust and networking bonds between individual researchers.
- Establishes ground rules for positive and supportive feedback.
- Further familiarises researchers with one another's proposals.
- Highlights specific areas in which the researchers can assist one another.

The peer-assist session can be divided into two sessions giving researchers time to go away and reflect on issues and/or read proposals in order to give more considered advice and guidance to their peers.

Giving Feedback

Effective feedback involves two-way communication between the person who gives the feedback and the person who receives it. Negative feedback is information that says 'do less of this'. Positive feedback is information that says 'do more of this'. Feedback can be both verbal and non-verbal.

Source:
www.iifoc.org

> **Resources:**
> **Guidelines for Peer-Assist:** *www.commonknowledge.org/ userimages/resources_peer_assist_guidellines+.pdf*
> **Tools for Knowledge and Learning, Ramalingam 2006 (Chapter 20 – Peer Assist):** *www.odi.org.uk/rapid/publications/ Documents/KM_toolkit_web.pdf*

POTENTIAL WORKSHOP SESSIONS > **Role Play**

Social research involves working successfully with men, women and children both individually and in group settings, particularly at the grassroots. In a **Networked Research** setting this becomes even more essential as the aim is for communities to adopt the findings and evidence for their own advocacy purposes.

The researchers who are selected to participate in your **Networked Research** programme may not all have field research experience and so a role-play session can be an effective tool for practicing and improving these skills. If necessary this session can also be used to encourage a gender-sensitive approach. During the *Mobility and Health Preparatory Researcher Workshops* the participants acted the 'dos' and 'don'ts' of field research in a series of humorous role-plays. A plenary session was then used to make sure that everyone identified all the 'dos' and 'don'ts' and agreed upon them. For example the participants agreed that small focus groups should be gender disaggregated including the facilitators.

ORGANISING A SUCCESSFUL FIELD VISIT

The inclusion of a field visit in the agenda of the **Preparatory Researcher Workshop** fulfils a number of aims, it:

Mobility and Health Researcher Workshop field visit, Indonesia 2006: An informal interview with female doctors

- Enables the researchers to understand and grapple with the realities of field work.

- Helps the core team to identify gaps in the researchers' field work capacity.

- Helps the researchers to formulate and practice good interviewing techniques and questions.

- Engages local stakeholders in the programme.

- Motivates and inspires the researchers and core team with new knowledge in a new context.

It is important therefore that sufficient planning goes into this activity. The facilitator should review the field visit agenda with the local organising team prior to the commencement of the workshop to allow sufficient time to recommend changes. In addition:

- The field visit should have a clear agenda such as to test techniques or to find specific information.

- Professional translators should be employed rather than relying on local researchers.

- Smaller groups visiting different locations are preferable.

- Overestimate and allow for transportation times.

- The local organising team should visit the location well in advance to ask the permission of the local community and fully inform them of the objectives of the visit.

For more advice on planning successful field visits turn to page 48.

DEVELOPING DISSEMINATION AND ADVOCACY STRATEGIES

Establishing and pursuing a dissemination and advocacy strategy at the beginning of the programme will enable you to raise awareness of your research and increase local, national and international ownership of your

research outputs. Dissemination and advocacy should therefore feature
strongly on the agenda of your **Preparatory Researcher Workshop**
where two distinct strategies should be developed:

- An international dissemination and advocacy strategy that engages
the programme with the international development agenda.
(See page 42 for further exploration).

- Local and national level dissemination and advocacy strategies in
which the researchers develop individual plans to promote the research
and engage change makers in their own context. These strategies
should form a key component of the researchers' Terms of Reference.

FORMULATING AN EFFECTIVE ADVOCACY STRATEGY

What?
Clarify what change(s) you are trying to bring about, then
prioritise your advocacy objectives by asking:

- What is achievable and realistic?
- What is opportunistic? e.g. imminent changes in policies or
government?
- What is affordable in terms of the time and resources
available to you?

Who?
Who can bring about the change you seek? Techniques such as
Stakeholder Analysis or *Power Mapping* are useful tools that
could be used at the **Preparatory Researcher Workshop** to
enable the core team and researchers to identify and prioritise
potential advocacy targets.

Stakeholder Analysis
Use Stakeholder Analysis to identify individuals and institutions with an interest or 'stake' in the issue. Brainstorm
stakeholders and cross reference them according to their
influence and their interest in your issue. Those with high-
influence and high-interest are those that the programme
should prioritise engagement with. Stakeholders with high
interest but low influence are potential advocates for your
research outputs. *(see page 41). Resource: RAPID www.odi.org.uk/
rapid/Tools/Toolkits/Policy_Impact/Stakeholder_analysis.html*

Power Mapping
Power Mapping is a methodology for determining who you
need to influence, who can influence your target and whom
you can actually influence to set the wheels in motion.
It looks at networks of relationships and should help the
team to identify achievable routes through which they can
influence their priority decision makers. *Resource: http://www.
idealist.org/ioc/learn/curriculum/pdf/Power-Mapping.pdf*

Why and How?

What is the case you are making and how will you make it? Your case needs to be factoral, accurate, emotive and credible. It needs to tell a story, describe a problem and propose practical solutions. Use the time at the **Preparatory Researcher Workshop** to think about the types of materials that the researchers will need to collect during their research to enable them to develop engaging advocacy messages. For example:

- Stories from research subjects and participants (good quotes).
- Visual aids e.g. good quality informative photographs.
- Illustrative statistics.

Where and When?

Think strategically about where and when to deliver your messages for maximum affect. What events and opportunities exist through which you can reach your advocacy targets with well prepared materials. Discuss optimum times to make contact with different stakeholders. For example:

- Before developing the research they can be consulted for ideas and the prioritisation of issues.
- They can be involved with the development of the research design.
- They can be informants or participants in the collection or analysis of the research data.
- They can participate in the peer-review following the completion and initial documentation of the research.
- They can participate in the final Symposium and/or receive the final information outputs *(see Step 4)*.

It is up to you to decide when it is most appropriate to engage your targets but generally you should aim to include them as early as possible. *Source: adapted from IFRTD Waterways and Livelihoods Advocacy Toolkit and START Simple Toolkit for Advocacy Research Techniques, VSO, 2005*

> A seed fund for small advocacy activities will enable the researchers to maximise opportunities to engage key stakeholders from the beginning of their research.

> Don't ignore the media, they are powerful advocates who can work for – or against – your cause. Identify which print publications, TV and radio programmes are used by your advocacy targets and develop relationships with their journalists. Be concise, be creative, have an exciting angle and provide engaging human interest stories to support your arguments.

ENGAGING LOCAL STAKEHOLDERS

Some of the researchers in the *Mobility and Health Networked Research programme* have appointed local steering committees, consisting of several stakeholders, to provide inputs and guidance to their research and to maximise local ownership of the programme. These steering committees will meet regularly and help to facilitate awareness raising events such as workshops and community meetings as well as linking the researchers to wider networks including the local media and key decision makers.

For more information
on Outcome Mapping
and other network
monitoring tools see
www.odi.org.uk/
RAPID/Tools/Toolkits/
Communication/
tools.html

MONITORING AND EVALUATION

How do we evaluate the impact of our research and know if it is really
catalysing positive changes in development policy and ultimately the
lives of poor people? Attempting to monitor and evaluate the impact of
communicated research represents a huge challenge:

- How do we establish impact within the timescale of a funded
  research programme?
- How do we attribute change specifically to our research outcomes
  and their communication?
- How do we detect unexpected or secondary impacts?
- How do we differentiate long-term change from short-lived impacts?

These are questions that we have struggled with in evaluating the
impact of **Networked Research programmes**. One methodology that
has emerged and which we think could be usefully applied in this context is *Outcome Mapping*. *Outcome Mapping* is a Monitoring and
Evaluation tool that was developed by the International Development
Research Centre (IDRC) to characterise and assess 'contributions to development outcomes' rather than 'achievement of development impact'.
The methodology monitors and evaluates people. It defines outcomes
as changes in the behaviour, relationships, activities and actions of the
programme's boundary partners i.e. the groups, organisations and individuals that the programme works with directly. These outcomes can be
logically linked to the programme and can be expected to enhance the
possibility of development impacts, without claiming direct attribution.

Application of the *Outcome Mapping* methodology to a **Networked
Research** programme could be achieved through incorporation into the
international and local level advocacy strategies *(see page 34)*. Through
processes such as *Stakeholder Analysis* and *Power Mapping* the core
team and researchers will already be establishing a picture of the people
with whom they anticipate direct interaction and opportunities for influence. This knowledge will facilitate the selection of boundary partners for
the *Outcome Mapping* process. Rather than being monitored and evalu-
ated from outside, the research team design the monitoring and evaluation framework and assess themselves as the programme progresses. The
process is participative, empowering and motivating as the researchers
and core team can see the impact of their work from the outset.

DEVELOPING THE RESEARCH GUIDANCE MANUAL

The *Research Guidance Manual* is the collaborative output from the
workshop(s), it brings together:

- The analytical research framework.
- Common terminology (e.g. a glossary).
- The Terms of Reference for the researchers.
- The international advocacy strategy.

- Local and national level advocacy strategies for individual researchers.

It provides background information, guidelines and instructions for designing, planning, undertaking and writing up the required field and desk research. In addition it outlines milestones, gives guidance on using the electronic networking tools (website, discussion list) and provides overall reporting information relevant to the programme. The **Manual** serves as an addendum to the letters of agreement or contracts signed by the participating researchers with the organising network.

MOBILITY AND HEALTH RESEARCH GUIDANCE MANUAL

The *Mobility and Health* programme researchers formulated their Research Guidance Manual through three regional **Preparatory Researcher Workshops** in Uganda, Indonesia and Mexico. It includes:

A conceptual framework.

Agreed guidelines for disaggregating data.

Agreed definitions of field and desk work with a statement of the required balance.

Principles of working with communities.

Ideas for advocacy activities.

Guidelines for gender sensitivity.

An extensive and detailed check-list of information/data to collect.

Reporting obligations and formats.

A timeline with milestones.

Guidelines for accessing and editing the team website and using the electronic discussion list.

See: *www.ifrtd.gn.apc.org/h_mob/about/research_ guidance_manual.php*

Other great resources with guidance on monitoring and evaluating networks:

'Measuring while you Manage. Planning, Monitoring and Evaluating Knowledge Networks' by H Creech, IISD, 2001. *www.iisd. org/pdf/2001/net works_evaluation.pdf*

'Participation, Relationships and Dynamic Change: New Thinking on Evaluating the Work of International Networks' M Church et al. 2003. *www.ucl.ac.uk/dpu/ publications/work- ing%20papers%20pdf/ WP121(i).pdf*

REFINING RESEARCH PROPOSALS

Following the **Preparatory Researcher Workshop(s)** the researchers will be given the opportunity to revise their proposals to take on board e new information they have received and the instructions from their search Guidance Manual. Allow sufficient time for thoughtful nges and translations where appropriate. Final proposals should be red via the electronic discussion list with their peers.

3.0

STEP 3 | RESEARCH PHASE

3.1 CAPACITY BUILDING AND PEER SUPPORT

Once the researchers return to the field to carry out their research they should be able to look to their new research community for support, guidance, inspiration and motivation.

The core team should be alert to the individual needs of each researcher. The channels through which they can provide support in an international context might include:

1. **Walk-in clinics**
   Scheduled support windows during which specific members of the core team are available for questions and discussions. Clinics should be advertised in advance and various communication channels used to suit the needs of different researchers, for example:

Photo courtesy of Paul Starkey

Researchers are now back in the field

- Telephone or Skype calls.

- Skype/Yahoo/MSN instant messenger.

- Use of the programme's electronic discussion list.

Following each clinic the core team member(s) involved should feed salient issues back to the wider team via the electronic discussion list.

Allow plenty of time for researchers to obtain the research permits and ethical permissions required in order to carry out their field work.

2. **Support visits**
Face-to-face visits made during the course of the research. They are most likely to be in response to specific capacity requirements that cannot be addressed via other forms of communication. They could also become necessary for reasons of conflict resolution, or to support researchers engaged in local or national level advocacy or dissemination activities.

The peer support process encouraged by the **Networked Research Approach** generates a continuous South to South dialogue that negates potential research hierarchies, encourages ownership of the research programme, and builds capacity and confidence within the research team. The core team can help to motivate a spirit of peer support by facilitating;

1. **An ethos of proactive networking on the electronic discussion list**
Researchers should not wait until they have a question or a problem to make contact with the wider team. Rather they should be encouraged to share new findings, successful initiatives, or new research tools e.g. a draft set of interview questions. This will motivate and inspire their peers!

2. **Exchange visits between researchers**
This can be particularly valuable where there are synergies between research topics, complementarities in research capacities (strong or weak) or where researchers share common advocacy targets. This will of course be subject to available resources.

Although the use of the electronic discussion list is encouraged for the purposes of continual learning and transparency it should be made clear to researchers that they can communicate directly with the core team and/or each other directly, when they feel it is appropriate.

Value diversity
Differences in culture, gender and professional orientation may manifest in different perspectives and ways of working. The **Networked Research Approach** values diversity and this should be reflected in the communications among the programme team at all times.

CHALLENGES

The demands placed on the researchers by the **Networked Research** process can be challenging. Networking (despite its rewards) can be time consuming and even intimidating. Participants in the *Mobility and Health Networked Research programme* voiced concerns regarding the time it will take to keep up to date with the electronic discussion list and other programme related communications. They also mentioned concerns regarding the quality of their research in comparison to other more experienced researchers.

Language is a major challenge. It is important to remember that the common denominator languages that are often used e.g. French, English, Spanish, may not be the mother tongue of many participants.

These challenges will manifest in:

- Misunderstandings.
- Delayed responses.
- Hesitancy to enter discussions, particularly online.

3.2 MONITORING

During the research phase the core team should monitor research milestones to ensure that the programme remains on schedule. A quick and easy way to keep an eye on progress is to initiate **monthly or bi-monthly reports** via the programme electronic discussion list. These should be made by each researcher and each member of the core team to ensure a 360 degree monitoring process. The reports do not have to be time consuming, just a brief statement of progress, the sharing of new experiences and tools, and where relevant, raising new issues or concerns.

Another possibility is a **Mid-programme Researcher Workshop**. Participants in IFRTD's **Networked Research** programmes have often requested a mid term review workshop. To date the funding has not been available but the requests are testament to the high value researchers have placed on opportunities for face-to-face networking. If the funds are available and your research phase is greater than 18 months in length this may be the perfect antidote to mid-research blues and an opportunity to review progress against milestones.

Engaging local stakeholders

3.3 ADVOCACY

The researchers and the core team should use the research phase to fine tune and kick-start the advocacy strategy that they developed at the **Preparatory Researcher Workshop.**

ENGAGING FUTURE ADVOCATES

As the researchers build their own localised research networks, comprising local stakeholders and decision makers, they will refine and build upon their original *Stakeholder Analysis* and *Power Mapping* to build a clearer picture of their advocacy allies, intermediaries and targets. At this stage they should also start to make a note of those people who are willing to be future advocates for the issue(s). Encourage the researchers to:

- Keep a file for contacts throughout the programme.

- Identify those people within the file who would be interested in advocacy.

- Ask and keep a list of how these people like to be contacted – phone, visit, email.

- Keep in touch – be proactive, set up meetings, hold events, keep these people interested and involve them in the advocacy strategy.

- Add a link to the programme website to their email signature.

- Promote the programme through their organisations and other networks.

Source: Adapted from START, Simple Toolkit for Advocacy Research Techniques, www.vso.org.uk

The core team should be alert for opportunities to promote the research programme at regional and international level. Such opportunities could include:

- The submission of preliminary research findings to conferences via academic papers and presentations.

- The distribution of promotional materials at appropriate events e.g. flyers, exhibition stands, posters, videos/dvds *(see Annex II)*.

- Requesting and facilitating a panel on your research issue at appropriate conferences.

- Writing pieces for newsletters, bulletins and journals.

- Initiating discussions on electronic discussion lists.

- Writing media friendly articles and press releases for dissemination at local, national, regional and international level – consider print, online, radio and TV.

The core team should divide these opportunities and responsibilities amongst the wider team.

3.4 REPORT WRITING AND PEER REVIEW

Researchers often start to write-up their findings too late. The important lesson here is to allow plenty of time and to actively seek feedback from peers both within and outside of the network. Initiating a peer review process for the final reports/case studies is a practical way for the network to self-regulate the quality of its outputs. If feedback is given positively and constructively this process will:

- Acknowledge the professional expertise residing within each of the researchers.

- Provide a safe environment in which to make mistakes.

- Contribute to the overall performance of the team.

Again language is a consideration. Where resources allow, researchers should be encouraged to write-up their research in their preferred language. Plenty of time must then be allowed for translation to enable peer-review and review by the core team.

4.0
STEP 4 | IMPACT AND SUSTAINABILITY

Synthesising and communicating your research findings will enable you to:

- Identify your key research messages.
- Articulate and advocate clear recommendations for policy and practice.
- Widen the Community of Practice interested in and taking ownership of your research issue(s).
- Highlight remaining research gaps and/or areas that require more in-depth exploration.

4.1 RESEARCHER SYNTHESIS WORKSHOP

- SYNTHESIS
- **LEARNING**
- DISSEMINATION
- **COLLABORATION**
- ADVOCACY
- **INFORMATION OUTPUTS**
- SUSTAINING MOMENTUM

The **Researcher Synthesis Workshop** is the opportunity for all the researchers to place their completed research in the context of the wider programme, and to participate in the feedback, synthesis and analysis of the research findings. This workshop should also draw out recommendations applicable to local, national and international situations.

It is important from the perspectives of capacity building, research integrity and advocacy that the final analysis and prioritisation of issues comes from the researchers themselves. Through this process:

- Knowledge, ideas and opportunities will be exchanged between researchers.
- The researchers will see and understand their contribution to the international development agenda.
- Their analytical capacity will be strengthened.
- They will be motivated to use the programme findings to evidence their own advocacy activities.

The core team should make a preliminary analysis and synthesis of the research findings for the purpose of gaining an oversight of the findings, briefing the **Synthesis Workshop** and **Final Symposium** facilitators and publicising the final **Final Symposium**. However they should not pre-determine discussions at the **Synthesis Workshop** and should be prepared to 'throw-out' any preconceptions they might have formed in order to absorb new, possibly very different, perspectives and priorities. For this reason alone an external facilitator for the **Synthesis Workshop** is a must.

Timing

Maximise resources and build on momentum by scheduling your **Synthesis Workshop** just prior to the **Final Symposium**. This will enable the entire team to prepare and finetune the agenda of the Symposium, taking ownership and responsibility for the impact of the overall programme.

This is also an opportunity to 'capacity-build' presentation skills. Encourage the researchers to bring scanned photographs and other visual aids to the workshops for this purpose.

SUGGESTED WORKSHOP OBJECTIVES

☐ Share individual case study findings.

☐ Identify synergies and disconnects between the case studies.

☐ Examine your overall research findings in the context of international development targets e.g. Millennium Development Goals, Poverty Reduction Strategies.

☐ Explore gaps between your research findings and current development policy and practice at local, national and international levels.

☐ Formulate clear research messages for local, national, regional and international audiences.

☐ Identify which case studies present the strongest evidence to support these messages.

☐ Report on advocacy progress (both researchers and core team).

MAXIMISE SHARING

Our experience has been that there is a wealth of information to share at the **Synthesis Workshop** and simply not enough time. Ask your researchers to bring videos, DVDs, and photo displays, and schedule optional evening or lunch time sessions.

CROSS POLLINATING CONCEPTUAL THOUGHT

Networked Research facilitates the migration of conceptual thinking, in particular through South-South exchange.

For example during the *Balancing the Load Networked Research Programme (see Annex I)* participating researchers from Bangladesh argued that 'mobility needs to be seen as a human right for women'. This concept was picked up again by a researcher from Senegal during the *Integrating Gender into World Bank Financed Transport Programs* programme who shared a 'think piece' on the topic via the IFRTD website. More recently the *Ethiopia Forum for Rural Transport and Development* hosted a national workshop that aimed to sensitise stakeholders on the rights of citizens to access and mobility, and the right to life as it relates to transport. A key output of this workshop was the formation of a Civil

Society Committee to discuss and present suggestions to the relevant authorities for the improvement of transport services in relation to the mitigation of the spread of HIV/AIDS and with respect to human rights.

INTERNATIONAL OR FINAL SYMPOSIUM

The overall goals of your **Final Symposium** will be to 'affect change' and to 'sustain momentum'. The completed research phase has put in place an evidence base, a Community of Practice and the first layers of an advocacy strategy. Now is the time to build upon this foundation by:

- Sharing the programme's key research messages with a wider audience.

- Engaging new faces with the Community of Practice.

- Further cross-pollinating knowledge and experience.

- Reviewing the synthesis of the research findings and the recommendations made.

- Encouraging all participants to apply the research findings to their own context.

- Formulating achievable and sustainable advocacy and implementation strategies.

WHO SHOULD PARTICIPATE?

This **Symposium** is a vital opportunity to strategically increase the audience for your research findings. Participants will include the existing researchers, the core team, plus other interested and invited stakeholders and change makers.

Who you invite will have a strong influence on the outcomes of the **Symposium** and ultimately the impact and sustainability of your research messages. The *Balancing the Load* programme held two **Final Symposiums**, one in Africa and one in Asia. In Asia a strong media presence enabled the **Symposium** to take on a very strategic communications and advocacy focus. Meanwhile in Africa there was almost no media representation but a stronger participation of key personnel from donor institutions. This resulted in a visible shift within these institutions towards prioritising gender in subsequent transport programmes.

How you organise the participation at your **Symposium** will depend to some extent upon the resources available to you and the level of interest you expect the event to generate. It is also important to consider:

- Will you charge participation fees?

- Will you sponsor participants (if so, with what criteria?)
- How will you select participants if over-subscribed?

  Remember to allow plenty of time to:

- Consult with the research team on potential invitees.
- Advertise the **Symposium** and receive applications.
- Send special invitations to decision makers that you would like to see at the event.

In particular the researchers should be encouraged to identify and invite their own key advocacy targets or their intermediaries. Local TV, radio and print journalists should also be invited to maximise coverage and exposure for both the local researchers and the international programme.

Local television crew interviewing participants at the Waterways and Livelihoods Symposium

SYMPOSIUM LOCATION

The location of the **Symposium** is also a strategic opportunity. With your researchers and core team identify:

1. **Are there any existing events that coincide with your timeline that you can 'piggy-back' your symposium to?** The advantages of this are that you will increase the profile of your event and therefore your research, and it may increase the likelihood of participation from certain stakeholders. For example the *Mobility and Health international Networked Research programme* seeks to attach its Final Symposium to a health sector conference for the purpose of attracting participation from health sector organisations.

2. **Do any of the researchers wish to host the Symposium for the purposes of local or national level advocacy?** For example the

International Symposium of the IFRTD *Waterways and Livelihoods Networked Research programme* was hosted by the Indonesian researchers in Pontianak, West Borneo. This was a strategic decision designed to raise the profile of rural waterways issues within the Kalimantan region. The **Symposium**, attended by the local media as well as local government officials, opened doors for a dialogue with the regional government to address rural water transport issues. Since the **Symposium** the Indonesian researchers have continued to push for the inclusion of water transport in transport planning.

SYMPOSIUM ORGANISATION AND FACILITATION

The format of the **Symposium** should maximise opportunities for participants to get involved and to share their experiences. There are many good facilitation techniques that you can use. We have already described some in Step 2 *(see page 30)*. A combination of these and other approaches could be used, for example action reviews or small debates – two people defending different positions on an issue can be fun and helps in the exploration and understanding of issues and different stakeholder perspectives. It is important to keep the agenda relaxed, informal and to avoid lengthy presentations.

WATERWAYS AND LIVELIHOODS

The three day International Symposium for the *Waterways and Livelihoods programme* was designed as a knowledge sharing and influencing event. Only the first day was spent presenting the research, for the remaining two days participants worked in groups to design an 'influencing strategy' that would promote rural water transport more widely. They identified what changes need to be made to tackle the invisibility of rural water transport, and by whom. They looked at the actions they wanted their targets to take in order to affect the desired changes and the messages that they should develop to prompt these actions.

THE SOCIAL SIDE

Opportunities for face-to-face networking are important for the sustainability of the Community of Practice. Personal contact and social interaction leads to satisfaction and a sense of belonging which in turn leads to commitment and increased engagement. Ensure that the symposium maximises opportunities for networking and small group interaction between participants.

Refreshment Rules
One break in the morning and one in the afternoon both of at least 30 minutes, serving small snacks or fruit. Lunch should be 60 to 90 minutes depending if it is a buffet or served food. These times should never be shortened – in many cultures socialising accompanies eating and these are vital networking opportunities.

Useful resource:
A useful guide for planning and organising conferences that bring together a diverse range of people (from activists to academics) in an informal environment to learn from and influence one another.

www.worldcarfree. net/members/ manual.php

Field Visit Questions
Structured questions should be avoided. A range of open ended questions can be used to encourage the various stakeholders to talk about the issues of most concern to them.

SYMPOSIUM FIELD VISIT

A field visit should provide the contextual reality to support your research messages. Ensure that it adds value to the discussions and takes place as an integral part of the Symposium agenda, rather than as an optional add-on.

Field visits can be great learning opportunities for participants but very disruptive for the hosting communities. Ensure that:

- Each community is visited by only a small group.
- The objectives of the field visit are clearly articulated and understood by your host(s).
- Your hosts are able to ask questions of the Symposium participants.
- The same 'dos' and 'don'ts' of working with communities during field research are applied.

Time should be allocated in the agenda on the day preceding the field visit to explain the objectives, logistics and methodology for the visit.

Participants should receive:

- Background information on the area to be visited including a map.
- Logistical information – what to wear, what to bring, times of departure etc.
- A summary of the day's objectives and expected outputs.

Time should also be allocated for participants to synthesise and feedback their field visit findings. The field visit should not be held on the last day as that would prevent valuable lessons from being shared and incorporated into the workshop outcomes.

For more guidance on the planning and organisation of field visits see *www.ifrtd.org/new/about/workshops.php*

Simultaneous translation
It's expensive but worth it! Without it participants will not fulfil their true potential in terms of contributing to and learning from the event.

REALITY CHECK

For many of the participants whose jobs keep them inside offices and separate from the people whose lives are affected by the policies they make, the field trip is a significant 'reality check'. One such participant in the *Waterways and Livelihoods Networked Research programme* commented that a concrete outcome of the Symposium was "finding out that the perceptions and attitudes of rural communities are important in gaining acceptance of water transport options, and that they can be emotional rather than logical responses".

OPTIONAL AND SPECIAL INTEREST SESSIONS

Some programme time, perhaps in the early evening(s), should be set aside for optional meetings and special interest groups. Some participants may wish to complement the broader aims of the Symposium discussions with detailed analysis or planning with colleagues working in similar fields or with similar priorities/concerns.

Sometimes by announcing these networking opportunities early in the programme it can set a precedent and lead to suggestions for further special sessions. These should be encouraged as they may lead to subsequent collaboration. *Source: Starkey P, 2004.*

4.3 INFORMATION OUTPUTS

Symposium
Resources
• Case Study Reports
  and Summaries
• Research programme
  Synthesis
• Policy
  Recommendations
• Field trip back-
  ground information

As with traditional research, **Networked Research** programmes produce physical outputs based upon the research findings. However these are audience focused and wherever possible not pre-determined by the research proposal or donor contract. Flexibility should be written in to the initial contract to allow for the development of research outputs that are responsive to the needs and recommendations of the programme as it develops.

WATERWAYS AND LIVELIHOODS
During the course of the *Waterways and Livelihoods* programme it became apparent that one of the main issues across the board was a lack of positive perception and overall visibility for rural water transport among development and transport policymakers. However the researchers and Symposium participants expressed their limitations in taking the new evidence forward in a meaningful way to influence decision-makers. In response the *Waterways and Livelihoods* core team developed an *Advocacy Toolkit* which included advice on simple advocacy activities and also isolated key policy messages drawn from the research findings.

Information products should be synthesised and packaged for different target audiences, for example:
• Policy briefs for decision makers.
• A book presenting the case studies and synthesis for other researchers.
• Papers for presentation at academic conferences.
• Toolkits with practical or technical recommendations for implementers.
• Workshop and Symposium reports for donors showing results and impact.
• Promotional materials for awareness raising e.g. videos, posters, brochures, leaflets *(see Annex II)*.

Ensure that sufficient time is allowed for the planning, preparation and production of information products. All too often information outputs are de-prioritised and the Symposium is seen as the end of the project.

The funding or facilitating organisation should not place any institutional ownership on the knowledge generated by **Networked Research** programmes. Attempts to copyright or own the outputs of **Networked Research** would in fact undermine the approach's core values of peer learning, South-South exchange and action oriented research.

Researchers are encouraged by the approach to find avenues to utilise and disseminate the programme outputs over and above those planned and funded within the original research proposal.

Tip: Include a budget line for ad-hoc dissemination and advocacy opportunities that researchers can apply to for funding. For example seed funding for national workshops, and/or local language publications.

Tip: Involve local NGOs and CBOs who have the best experience in working with communities, and translate publications back into local languages or disseminate your findings via the local media e.g. community radio.

SUSTAINING MOMENTUM

The Communities of Practice or networks that emerge from **Networked Research** are the key to building upon and sustaining the momentum that has been built up throughout the course of the programme. These communities have the potential to:

- Push the issues forward and keep the debate current.
- Provide mutual support and peer review.
- Establish a source of shared expertise on the focal issue.
- Provide an ongoing platform from which to advocate for change.
- Identify new opportunities for pushing the communities agenda forward.

There was originally an assumption that increased ownership of the issues will lead to strategic advocacy activities from strong emerging networks engaged at both the local and international level. The observed reality however has been that advocacy activities in the long term are ad-hoc and are at their strongest locally and nationally. The GATNET Gender and Transport community that emerged from the *Integrating Gender into World Bank Financed Transport Programs* programme is the exception to this rule having developed into a recognised community on the international stage *(see page 3)*.

VARIOUS FACTORS AFFECT THE SUSTAINABILITY
OF NETWORKED RESEARCH COMMUNITIES

In the years immediately following the *Balancing the Load* programme, there was a visible uptake of gender issues within the transport sector. The UN Commission for Africa initiated a series of gender and transport studies using the researchers from the **Networked Research** programme. The Sub Saharan Africa Transport Policy Program's Rural Travel and Transport Program (RTTP) initiated the Gender and Rural Transport Initiative (GRTI) to support practical pilot projects in the region, and several of the *Balancing the Load* case studies were used by the World Bank for gender and transport awareness raising programmes. The impetus for many of these Bank-led activities came from the World Bank's Gender and Transport Thematic Group, and when it wound down gender once again seemed to fall off the radar.

Although several of the *Balancing the Load* community of researchers continued to push the gender and transport agenda in other forums and Communities of Practice. It has been the emergence of a fresh community of practitioners from the *Integrating Gender into World Bank Financed Transport Programs* programme that has really revived the issue on the international agenda. This community has grown rapidly and is now a recognised source of expertise on the issue of gender and transport (see GATNET on page 3).

The *Waterways and Livelihoods* community, despite having an electronic discussion list that was opened to the public and attracted many new members, became relatively dormant about one year after the completion of the research programme. Feedback from the community, solicited by the IFRTD Secretariat, revealed that many participants are still engaged with the issues at a local and national level. For example the Indonesian researchers continue to advocate for the inclusion of waterways issues at national policy level and in Colombia participants in the **Final Symposium** formed a local network, the Orinoquia Forum for Rural Water Transport that continues to pursue the issues locally.

At an international level the research has led to some level of acceptance of the neglect of rural waterways in the transport sector and the DFID initiated global Transport Knowledge Partnership (gTKP) includes rural water transport in its mandate. However half hearted interest by the international community has meant that many of the interesting practical follow-up initiatives recommended by the programme participants, such as artisanal exchanges to cross-pollinate boat technologies and the translation of the programme outputs to french for dissemination in West and Central Africa, could not be pursued despite a clear demand.

Overleaf we have tried to isolate some of the factors that have helped the GATNET community to establish a greater longevity than its predecessors:

In development a typical Community of Practice comprises a group of practitioners focusing on a specific subject field, facilitating sharing of information and skills. They can be members of the same organisation. However, the great strength of such communities is that, enabled by new ICTs in the form of groupware, they are able to facilitate contact between practitioners working in different organisations in different parts of the world."

Cummings, S and A van Zee, 2005.

FACTORS THAT FACILITATE SUSTAINABILITY:

- Recognition from established institutions.
- Meaningful participation of members in the network.
- Meaningful participation of the network in international discourses.
- Institutional support (however minor) to facilitate the electronic discussion group and/or other communication.
- Members put time (however minor) on making inputs to the list to motivate discussions.
- Small activities that require few resources other than members time e.g. Virtual Forums with rotating moderators.
- A sense of community and identity.
- Autonomy - institutional support should not compromise network autonomy.
- Keeping organisation simple - no pressure to adopt a bureaucratic structure or seek funding as an entity.

FACTORS THAT INHIBIT SUSTAINABILITY:

- Lack of facilitated communication.
- Lack of a long term sense of community and identity.
- The issue around which the community is mobilised is de-prioritised by institutions.
- Core members lose interest, change jobs, drift away.
- No joint initiatives.
- No emerging challenges for the group to deal with (could be because of the deprioritisation of the issue, or positively, if the advocacy has succeeded in mainstreaming the ideas).

With the *Mobility and Health* programme we will see for the first time a **Networked Research programme** that has incorporated advocacy activities from the beginning. The core team is seeking resources for a seed fund to support researchers with the advocacy and follow-up initiatives that will enable them to build upon the programme outputs and deliver real change in policy and practice.

when I undertook
a study on 'Integrating Gender in World Bank Transport
Programmes' way back in 2003. This was a refreshing
experience. The methodology was discussed and agreed upon
in a participatory manner and I was supported throughout the
study. This is the difference. Knowing that there is somebody,
somewhere who is going through a similar exercise, perhaps
experiencing similar challenges. Knowing that there is at least
someone available for you to consult whenever you wish, is very
inspiring. Another unique aspect of Networked Research is due
to the frequency and intensity of interaction, a 'sisterhood'
is developed amongst the researchers and the coordination
team. This is how GATNET was born.

The GATNET 'sisterhood' has outlived the original research
process but the networking continues. GATNET has expanded
from the original 10 or so members to the current 100 plus.
What keeps GATNET alive is the committed membership who,
whenever the need arises, organise around an issue. Sometimes,
these issues are identified by the members. Many times though
they are identified by associated organisations such as the
IFRTD and the World Bank. I see this institutional support
as playing a facilitative role.

What I see happening is a quiet revolution in the transport
sector. GATNET is being heard. It is slowly but surely gaining
legitimacy in an otherwise male dominated transport world.

APPENDICES

Networked Research in Practice

Balancing the Load was IFRTDs pioneering Networked Research programme. Between 1998 and 1999 the IFRTD brought together people working with groups of poor women in different countries in Asia and Africa and encouraged them to analyse their own context and experiences from the perspective of gender and mobility.

The 31 researchers included a team from the Self Employed Women's Association (SEWA) and the SEWA bank in Ahmedebad, India, an architect from Calcutta, two activists (one with links to a remote village in India and the other to tribal communities in India), staff of international NGOs in Sudan, Sri Lanka and Bangladesh, the coordinator of the Village Travel and Transport Programme in Tanzania, a government official and a transport safety professional from Uganda, a transport planner from the Centre for Scientific Research in South Africa, as well as independent consultants and academics from South Africa, Nigeria, Burkina Faso, Bangladesh, Nepal and the United Kingdom. More information: *www.ifrtd.org*

The Waterways and Livelihoods project was a smaller programme that aimed to raise the profile of rural waterways in the transport sector and among development planners, to increase its visibility as an issue, to contribute to new knowledge about the impact of rural water transport upon poor people's mobility and access needs, and to highlight its potential benefits for the environment. A team of researchers across Asia, Latin America, and Africa comprising development practitioners, government transport ministries, and university academics, identified locations in vulnerable areas where there is a significant incidence of poverty and where rural water transport is a sole or principal means of transport. The team of ten researchers gathered together in a workshop in Cambodia to formulate their common research methodology. The research culminated in a three day researcher workshop to synthesise findings in preparation for an international seminar. More information: *www.ruralwaterways.org*

Integrating Gender into World Bank Financed Transport Programs was a programme initiated by the World Bank in 2001 via the consultancy firm IC Net. The programme invited IFRTD to collaborate with its research phase and a Networked Research methodology was introduced. 10 researchers from 9 countries came together to formulate the research methodology. The programme struggled to come to terms with the Networked Approach which at times conflicted with the bureaucratic guidelines of the Bank. Ultimately however this programme gave birth to a strong and dynamic community of practice around gender and transport issues. More information: *www.dgroups.org/groups/worldbank/gatnet*

The Mobility and Health programme, initiated by IFRTD in 2005, aims to carry out 24 case studies across Asia, Latin America and Africa, exploring the existing and potential links between mobility and health, particularly in rural areas. This is the first time that IFRTD has carried out Networked Research simultaneously in three languages; English, French and Spanish.

Tools will be developed to enable transport professionals to include holistic health impact assessments and mitigation measures in the planning, design and implementation of transport interventions. The programme also aims to sensitise the health sector to health and mobility issues.
More information: *www.mobilityandhealth.org*

ANNEX II

The Public Face of a Networked Research Programme

The core team of the Mobility and Health Networked Research programme has developed a logo, an interactive tri-lingual website and an exhibition stand for display at conferences and events *(see below)*.

ANNEX III

Essentials for Facilitation

Facilitation in general:

☐ Clarify the background and context of the discussion.

☐ Ensure there is proper understanding and clarify misunderstandings.

☐ Look for concrete and practical examples illustrating the discussion.

☐ Caution people who do more that their fair share of talking and activate silent participants.

☐ Summarise discussions and try to distil essential issues.

☐ Stimulate discussions by asking questions.

☐ Address different opinions and positions by making differences transparent.

☐ Try to settle potential conflicts.

☐ Remind people about the rules of conversation.

☐ Address or clarify the feelings of participants in the discussion.

☐ Raise awareness for cultural, social, religious or political differences and promote understanding.

Facilitation of face-to-face meetings, workshops or conferences:

☐ Visualise the discussions.

☐ Admit people to the floor.

☐ Carefully caution people who talk to much.

☐ Give feedback to the participants.

☐ Ensure good time management.

☐ Carry out a review of the workshop.

Source: Work the Net, GTZ, 2006.

USEFUL REFERENCES

Church M et al (2003) Participation, Relationships and Dynamic Change: New Thinking on Evaluating the Work of International Networks
www.ucl.oc.uk/dpu/publications/working%20papers%20pdf/WP121(i).pdf

Creech H (2001) Measuring while you Manage. Planning, Monitoring and Evaluating Knowledge Networks. IISD
www.iisd.org/pdf/2001/networks_evoluation.pdf

Cummings, S and A van Zee (2005) Communities of Practice and Networks: reviewing two perspectives on social learning. KM4D Journal 1(1): 8-22
www.km4dev.org/journal

Czuczman K (2006) A Networked Research Approach. IFRTD
www.ifrtd.org/new/about/nresearch.php

Egger U, Glueck M et al. (2006) Work the Net, A Management Guide for Formal Networks. GTZ
www.threads.ch/documentation/skatdacumentation.2006-06-30.4987952114/

Fernando P and Porter G (2002), Balancing the Load. Women, Gender and Transport, Zed Books, London & New York
www.ifrtd.org

IFRTD (1999) Balancing the Load, Proceedings of the Asia and Africa Regional Seminars on Gender and Rural Transport
www.ifrtd.org

KFPE (1998) Guidelines for Research in Partnership with Developing Countries – 11 Principles. Swiss Commission for Research Partnership with Developing Countries
www.kfpe.ch/key_activities/publications/guidelines/guidelines_e.php

Overseas Development Institute (ODI) Research and Policy in Development (RAPID)
www.odi.org.uk/RAPID/Index.html

Perkins N (ed) (2006) Proving our Worth: developing capacity for the monitoring and evaluation of communicating research in development. Healthlink
www.research4development.info/PDF/Articles/mande_summary.pdf

Starkey P, (January, 2004) Some thoughts on workshop organisation and methodology (draft)
www.ifrtd.org/new/about/workshops.php

Waterways and Livelihoods (2003) Resource for Promoting Improved Policy and Practice. IFRTD Secretariat.
www.ruralwaterways.org/gen/common/advocacy.pdf

Tweedie L (2005) START Simple Toolkit for Advocacy Research Techniques. VSO
www.eldis.ids.ac.uk/static/DOC21074.htm

USEFUL ONLINE RESOURCES

Blogs
An introduction to blogs and blogging.
www.en.wikipedia.org/wiki/Blog

Free online blog space.
www.blogger.com

Email Discussion Lists
Dgroups – Online platform for international teams (includes electronic mailing list). The following organisations are entitled to use Dgroups: Partner organisations or members of Bellanet, CGIAR, CTA, DFID, Hivos, ICA, ICCO, IICD, KIT, OneWorld,

UNAIDS, CIDA, Danida, FAO, IDRC, INASP, SNV, Sida, SDC, UNECA, and World Bank.
www.dgroups.org
Yahoo Groups and Google Groups – Free electronic mailing lists
www.groups.yahoo.com
www.groups.google.com

Online Workspace
Teamspace – Low cost and easy to use web portal.
www.teamspace.com

Free Image Resources
Photoshare – A service of the INFO programme, helping international non-profits to communicate health and development issues through photography. Images can be requested from an extensive photo database for non-profit educational use.
www.photoshare.org
The Flickr Creative Commons – A searchable public photo-sharing database. A proportion of images are available for free reproduction under 'creative commons' licenses.
www.flickr.com/creativecommons

Workshop Methodologies
World Café – Guidance on the World Café workshop technique.
www.worldcafe.com
Peer Assist – Guidelines.
www.commonknowledge.org/userimages/resources_peer_assist_guidellines+.pdf
www.odi.org.uk/rapid/publications/Documents/KM_toolkit_web.pdf
Guide to Planning and Organising Conferences.
www.worldcarfree.net/members/manual.php
International Institute for Facilitation and Consensus (IIFAC) –
Resources and publications relating to workshop facilitation.
www.iifac.org

Advocacy Tools
Stakeholder Analysis.
www.odi.org.uk/RAPID/Tools/Toolkits/Policy_Impact/Stakeholder_analysis.html

Power Mapping
www.idealist.org/ioc/learn/curriculum/pdf/Power-Mapping.pdf

Other Useful Tools
Gantt Charts – Planning and scheduling projects.
www.ganttchart.com
Babel Fish – Online translation tool.
www.babelfish.altavista.com
Network Monitoring Tools
www.odi.org.uk/RAPID/Tools/Toolkits/Communication/tools.html
Skype – Voice over Internet Protocol enabling low cost or free telephone connections over the Internet plus instant messaging.
www.skype.com

YOUR FEEDBACK

The Networked Research Approach is a work in progress. From the pioneering Balancing the Load programme to the current Mobility and Health research, IFRTD has been refining and developing its interpretation of research in a network setting. We welcome your feedback on this guide and the issues it raises, particularly if you use a similar approach or are able to introduce some or all of the Networked Research Approach into your research practices. We look forward to hearing from you.

IFRTD

The International Forum for Rural Transport and Development known as IFRTD or 'The Forum' is a global network of individuals and organisations working together towards improved access and mobility for the rural poor in developing countries. It achieves this aim by identifying gaps in knowledge and capacity, promoting priority issues for change, supporting networking and new research, and pursuing a programme of advocacy work that will influence donors, policy makers and practitioners.

www.ifrtd.org

SKAT

Skat is an independent Swiss resource centre and consulting company working in the fields of development and humanitarian aid. Since 1978, Skat has provided technical expertise and management support to bilateral and multilateral development agencies, and non-governmental organisations. Skat participates in networks in many different roles; as a member, a facilitator, an organiser of workshops and conferences and also as a participant in working groups and applied research projects. In recent years, Skat has built up particular expertise in facilitating and managing networks.

www.skat.ch

Author
Kate Czuczman
IFRTD Secretariat
in collaboration with
Priyanthi Fernando,
Marinke van Riet &
Dr. Urs Karl Egger

Cover Illustration
'Stand on My
Shoulders'
& Design/Layout by
7th Floor

Printing by
Active Print
Management

Published by
IFRTD,
November 2006

www.ingramcontent.com/pod-product-compliance
Lightning Source LLC
LaVergne TN
LVHW011803070326
832902LV00031B/4652